I Contact with Self

Become now

notionpress.com

I Contact with Self

Become now

Kiran Phadnis

notionpress.com

Notion Press

Old No. 38, New No. 6
McNichols Road, Chetpet
Chennai - 600 031

First Published by Notion Press 2016

ISBN 978-93-86009-88-3

"Childful
Contemplation!"

Preface

Imagine—your house doorbell rings, you jolt out of the chair to open the door, only to see *yourself* at the doorstep waiting to be welcomed in. How would you feel?

After having tasted failure and success over the past many years, I was fortunate to be bestowed with the biggest gift from *life*—a powerful *pause* … a pause to ask my life some *truthful* questions. Not many get a chance in the rush, to accept this gift.

This book in my own little way is an effort to enable us to accept this gift from life. It is all about that moment and what unfolds thereafter. It's about *you* and *I*, about an open conversation with self.

The core weaving idea is to take a pause and have a party with friends within; beyond the "still noise" and "dynamic silence!"

Become now and let the journey unfold!

I would like to dedicate this book to my dear parents and wife, Manisha, who allowed me to dream and have always been of great support to me.

A *big thanks* to my dear parents, wife, children and friends for being the true source of inspiration and encouragement in this journey.

Those were the days... these are the days... and this is the moment!

There was this young teacher, who, one fine day, asked the kids at school, “What stops you from having all the fun in the class?”

Students said, “You!”

The teacher picked a bottle of water and splashed water on the students in the class saying, “I know you are full of it and you are known to have it all.” Within moments, there was a jubilant mood.

Later in the evening at an adult learning session, he asked the same question to the class.

Students said, “It’s not meant to be that way!”

The teacher again picked a bottle of water from a nearby table and splashed the water on himself and in a moment there was jubilation in the classroom.

Next day, the teacher was interacting with a few senior citizens in the nearby locality, and he asked them the same question.

The senior citizens said, “It’s our last lap and we do not really know why not,” and so saying one of them picked up a bottle of water and splashed water on himself and the teacher, and screamed on top of his voice saying,

"We wish we had done this a long time back with our lives!"

And there was a stark silence for a while in the classroom…

…and the *fun* began!

"The tunes of life said to my wishes that in all the act of design to shine, you have lost to listen to the very essence of our music. Embrace us and the music will embrace you beyond you!"

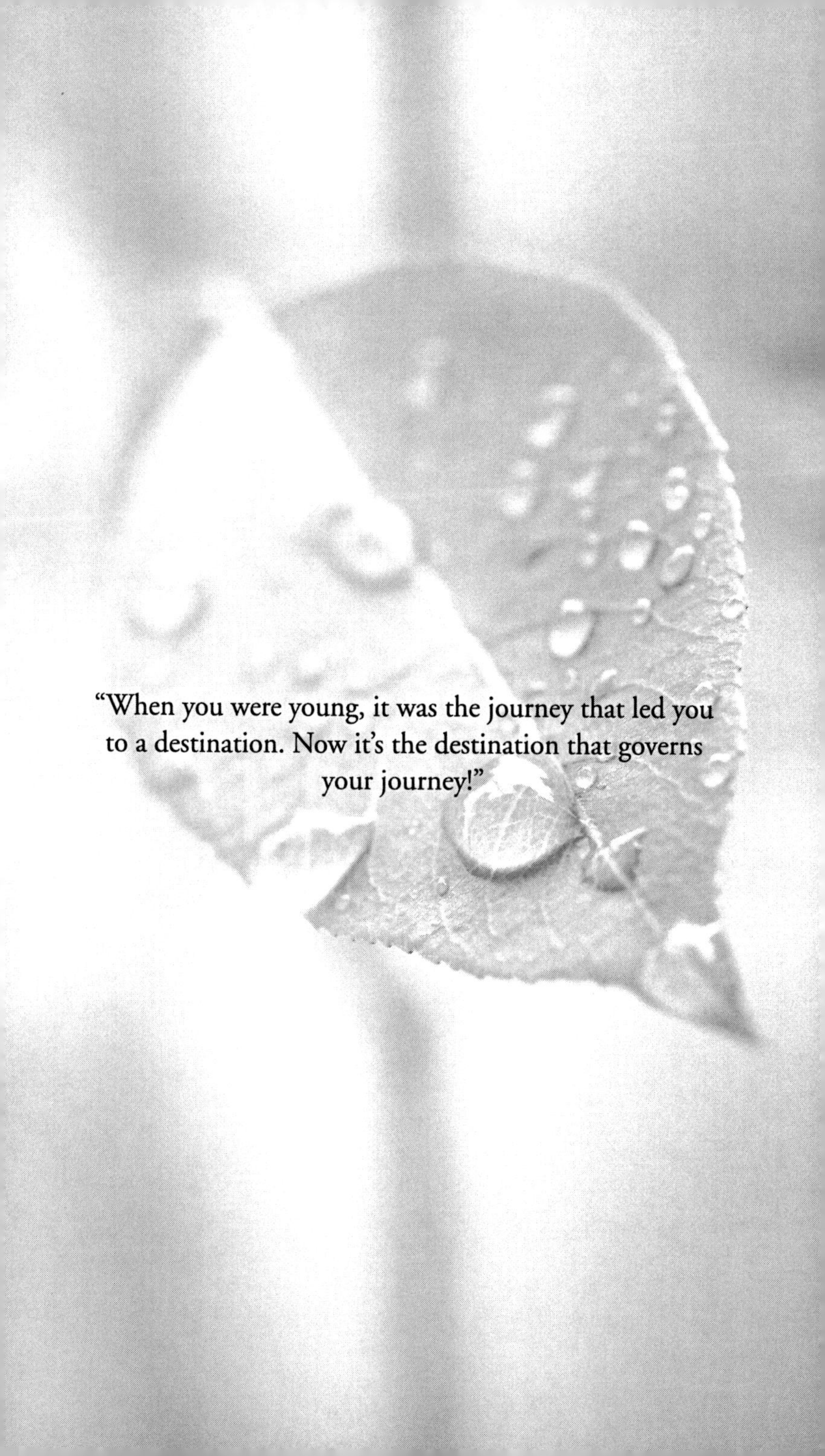

"When you were young, it was the journey that led you to a destination. Now it's the destination that governs your journey!"

"In the rush of 'how it should be,' you have shown an unfriendly gesture towards all the friends who want to make you win … the friends of the abundant you!"

"And I asked the child in me and it said: I always wanted to just play the game!"

It was during one of those early monsoon days when rain showered across the night with a fair amount of lightning and thunder.

"Wake up; wake up," he said and thud … as I woke up, there were huge sea waves swirling in my mind. For a minute I could only see myself standing with the mighty sea staring at me, and me staring at the horizon in oblivion. And there came the pat on my shoulder. I looked back in a shock, to find myself standing … and the alarm clock rang and I woke up to reality.

Those few moments were haunting me for a couple of weeks. Was it me, was it the aspiring me, was it the subconscious me, or was it just some crazy dream?

I was not able to understand what was happening. Who was it? It was difficult to understand whether the storm was within me or outside me. The more I thought, the more anxious I became. All I did then was to share it with friends in a way that it was received as a sane event. I had my own stories attached which did help me momentarily vent out. But then again in times when I was on my own, there were millions of thoughts, emotions and a blank state again!

All that kept me going was a faint belief that something new was around the corner. I had begun my inner journey of exploring self!

And the day arrived, Tuesday, 22 August, I had woken up and finished with the daily chores and there was a knock on the door, "Can I come in please?"

I had goose bumps. For forty years of my life, I was used to inviting guests; however here I was, for the first time inviting myself … my inner master. My truthful inner voice—the voice that had been with me all along the way. However, in the true sense, it had been a long time since I had lent my ear to. My master was carrying a wonderful gift with him—the gift of "silence."

It was weird, difficult and I was only experiencing a state of connecting and accepting the vastness of the universe. I could see three other unknown friends accompanying him. By the time I'd welcomed them in, with a sheer thought of being a bit lost and sceptical, they reached out and warmly greeted me and made themselves comfortable. Then, my inner master introduced me to them one by one—the child in you, the future you and the journey guide.

There was nothing that I could identify with, from the past. My inner master and his friends were dressed different, looked different and spoke different. Though they were different, I was feeling relaxed as they seemed at home. The beauty of the initial exchanges happened when, with all the differences, I was able to relate to everything that was going on.

The inner master then said, "If you feel like serving your guests with some questions or answers, you are more than welcome. If not, we are okay to leave. Anyway, meeting you is always a pleasure!"

Lie — Truth, lucky you! You are a free bird without any burden.

Truth — Lie, lucky you! I am nothing without you.
Unless one undresses me of you,
I cannot be visible.

Conscience Master — What lends me strength is an honest conversation between the two of you.

In conversation with the inner master…
"Feel it!"

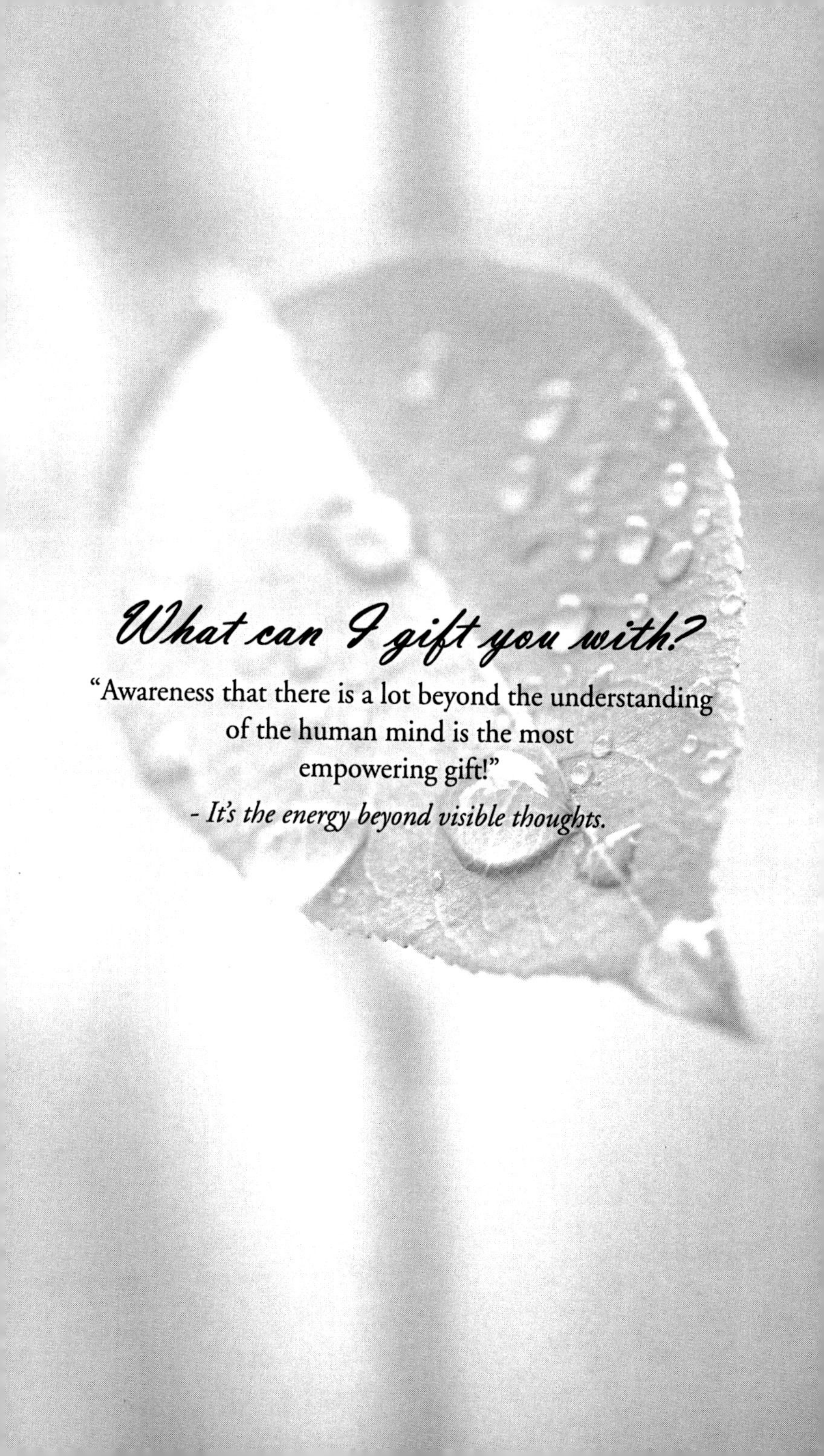

What can I gift you with?

"Awareness that there is a lot beyond the understanding of the human mind is the most empowering gift!"

- It's the energy beyond visible thoughts.

So, what are moments all about?

"Life is all about a moment between moments. The reason has been laid out already and all we do is find our place in it. When we do find it, we call it our moment. This becomes a new reason in the journey laid out already!"

- We live and write our story between moments.

How do you intend to guide me?

"We are able to find ourselves better not only within; but also in the energy scattered without. We do need a canvas to showcase the different colors of life!"

- The outside experience lends us with an eye to look within.

What is it that drives us?

"To find our self in everything around us is the beginning of life, but to find everything around within us is the true journey.

And to create an experience and help others is meaningful learning!"

- It's about the 'vastness within'.

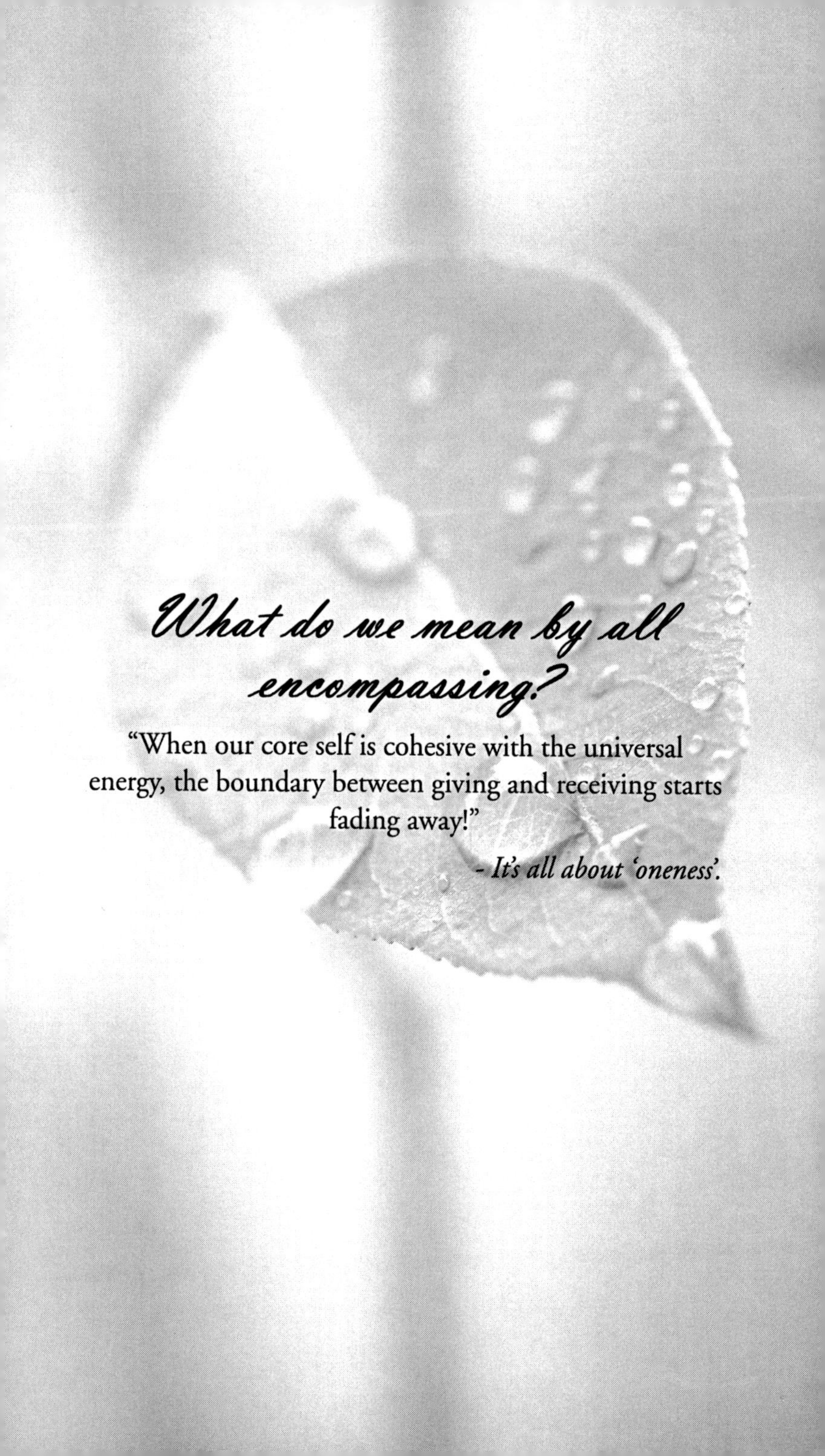

What do we mean by all encompassing?

"When our core self is cohesive with the universal energy, the boundary between giving and receiving starts fading away!"

- It's all about 'oneness'.

Should we ponder or wander?

"What is the color of your deeply embedded emotion and thought?"

- The problem lies in the question itself.

How does it matter anyway?

"If the color was to be visible, would you like to showcase it or hide it?"

- Something to ponder about!

But what should I do with the barrage of thoughts?

"To explore the unknown beauty beyond thoughts requires inking the mind differently!"

- Feed yourself with the belief in the beauty beyond.

What helps us truly detach and run faster?

"We are able to untie a few of our 'invisible knots' only when we get past our 'visible thoughts'!"

- New possibilities lie outside the present thought boundaries.

For years I have been a tourist in my own land. What does it take to be a traveler?

"The more you search for the truth; you are operating by design and less with the FLOW. The flow has no meaning attached. If at all it does, it is what manifests in the journey, which 'the traveler' is not concerned with anyway.

Everything that flows is out of the emptiness and into it.

It's a state that embraces the unknown and signifies abundance.

Before and beyond it is life, in between is what makes life!"

- *The abundance in the flow zone*

How does it help?

"A centered stillness within, comes from a deep rooted appreciation of the fact that the very essence of life is the 'FLOW!'"

- Stillness is the sound of silence!

Where do we find our strength?

"The inner purpose gets bolder from a fight within. The day this battle becomes second nature, you find the stronger you!"

- Be friends with or fight the demons within.

How?

"Detached to pain and attached to pleasure leads to attachment with pain and detachment with pleasure!"

- The more you run away, the more it will follow you.

What about tough times?

"We can sail through rough waters with strength, only when we acknowledge the fact that pain is 'essence-tial' to make the journey more 'meaning-full!'"

- Embracing pain turns it into a meaningful healer!

Around 3:00 PM, as I was serving my guests with questions, my inner master suggested that we take a stroll outside. I was not sure about the intent. However, I agreed, and in a few minutes, we stepped out. As we were walking down the road, we sighted a coffee shop at a distance and decided to visit it and sip a cup of coffee.

There were people of all ages around. As we settled and placed an order for coffee, with a smile on the face, he asked, "Do you hear the conversation going on amongst those four friends at the next table?"

We could faintly hear what each one was saying. It seemed like they were college friends, who had met up after ages.

One of them said, "I have had a tough journey after college. Life has not been fair with me. I didn't land up in a good job earlier and even today I feel I could have done much better." And at the end, he said, "Those were the days, good old college days!"

The second friend said, "Sad to hear that, luckily, life has been gracious with me and I was able to make it big in life with all the fame and success. Thanks to everyone who made it possible." And at the end, he also said, "Those were the days, good old college days!"

The third one said, "I am too lost to know whether I have failed or succeeded in life. It's the same old routine work day in and day out and I feel I have gotten numb to the way my life is headed." And at the end he too said, "Those were the days, good old college days!"

And, as he finished, the three of them saw their other friend, who until now was laughing his heart out, suddenly wearing a somber mood. In a moment, tears welled up in his eyes and he said, "It's been one hell of a ride for me. I lost my wife two years back, lost my job three months back, have two kids to take care of, and do not really know what's in store for me." And at the end he said, "This is the day and the moment!"

His friends were dumbstruck and didn't know how to respond. After a long silence, the fourth friend gathered himself and wearing a smile on his face said, "Sorry friends, but let's forget what we've lost or gained. What matters the most now is how we can make this reunion after ages a memorable one.

Let's party and have fun!"

And I found my answer!

Pain — Pleasure, lucky you! Everyone looks forward to being with you.

Pleasure — Pain, lucky you! You are the most learned of all. I am nothing without your awareness; always waiting for you to bring me to life.

Stillness Master — In the true sense, the essence lies in me being dressed with both of you.

Your empty reflective space... gift it!

PAINT YOUR CANVAS!

So it's "I" who is at fault?

"I guarded the 'I' with the 'eye' and got blindfolded. Let the self not consume one so much that others do not get a chance to experience it."

- It builds walls around your self.

How do we let the e-go?

"You can challenge the ego, only when you have played around with it
with awareness for a long time!"

- Being aware of the costs we pay, helps let go of it.

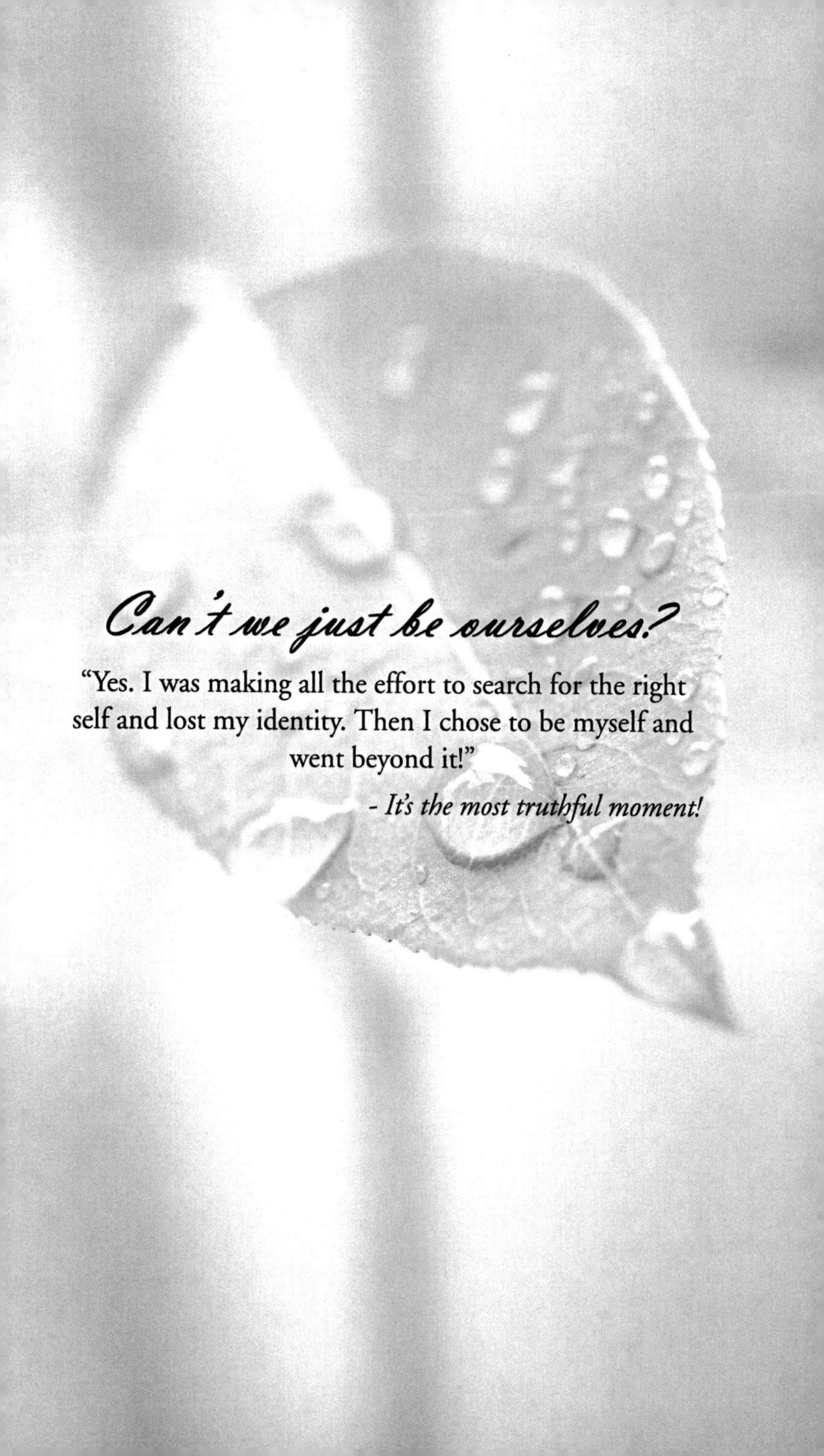

Can't we just be ourselves?

"Yes. I was making all the effort to search for the right self and lost my identity. Then I chose to be myself and went beyond it!"

- It's the most truthful moment!

How can we better understand self?

"When you move away from self, you truly come closer to it!"

- Else, we wear on blinkers of self.

What keeps us blinkered in relationships?

"I cannot see beyond 'who they are,' unless I go beyond 'who I am!'"

- We wear our own perceptual glasses.

Why are people so different from each other?

"Deep down within us, the so-called contrasting colors are actually one and the same. It's just that when they meet each other, they surface in different shades!"

- The internal dialog between emotions triggers our external responses.

What is the best way to get unstuck?

"The mind with a selfless desire is able to go beyond set boundaries!"

- Expectations restrict us from thinking beyond ourselves.

What about the pain of loss?

"True strength of detachment lies in being able to be so attached that you don't miss it when it has left you!"

- The strength of attachment helps you to move on.

Easier said than done, isn't it?

"True detachment is being willing to leave few questions unanswered!"

- It happens when our attachment does not question us.

When does fear creep in?

"When our dearest attachments are questioned and we are unwilling to budge!"

- Allow the thrill of life to answer all the questions.

What about being attached to our core values?

"They lend us strength and fear will never knock on their door!"

- They build inner cohesiveness.

My internal master took a pause and said,

"I sense that the storm within is making you restless. I will answer all your questions. Hold your horses and the rest will follow."

What makes for a true adventure?

"True adventure begins without the need to embrace reason. It stems out of the empty space!"

- True adventure embraces the abundance of the unknown.

Wouldn't we get lost without it?

"I found my inner compass only when I was lost on the way."

- The unknown drives us to be open to multiple directions.

What about clarity about the future?

"It is important. A compelling vision is the mirror of your dreams that reflects the image of the newer you!"

- The vision of the desired picture.

Then don't we need to wish strongly to find it?

"The unfound gets unfolded not when we want it, but when the flow finds it!"

- Do wish, however it helps to let the unfound find you.

Where does all that we wish stem from?

"We create our own experiences, as deep down, the possible future events are well written in our subconscious mind!"

- All that we strongly wish gets stored in the subconscious box.

What's wrong in being focused?

"Nothing's wrong. However, let the focused eye not be blinded to the abundance around!"

- Over focusing eyes become oblivious to things around.

But, doesn't our experience come in the way?

"The experience of the exploring mind is determined by its ability to flow without it!"

- Let the experience guide us, and not stifle creative options.

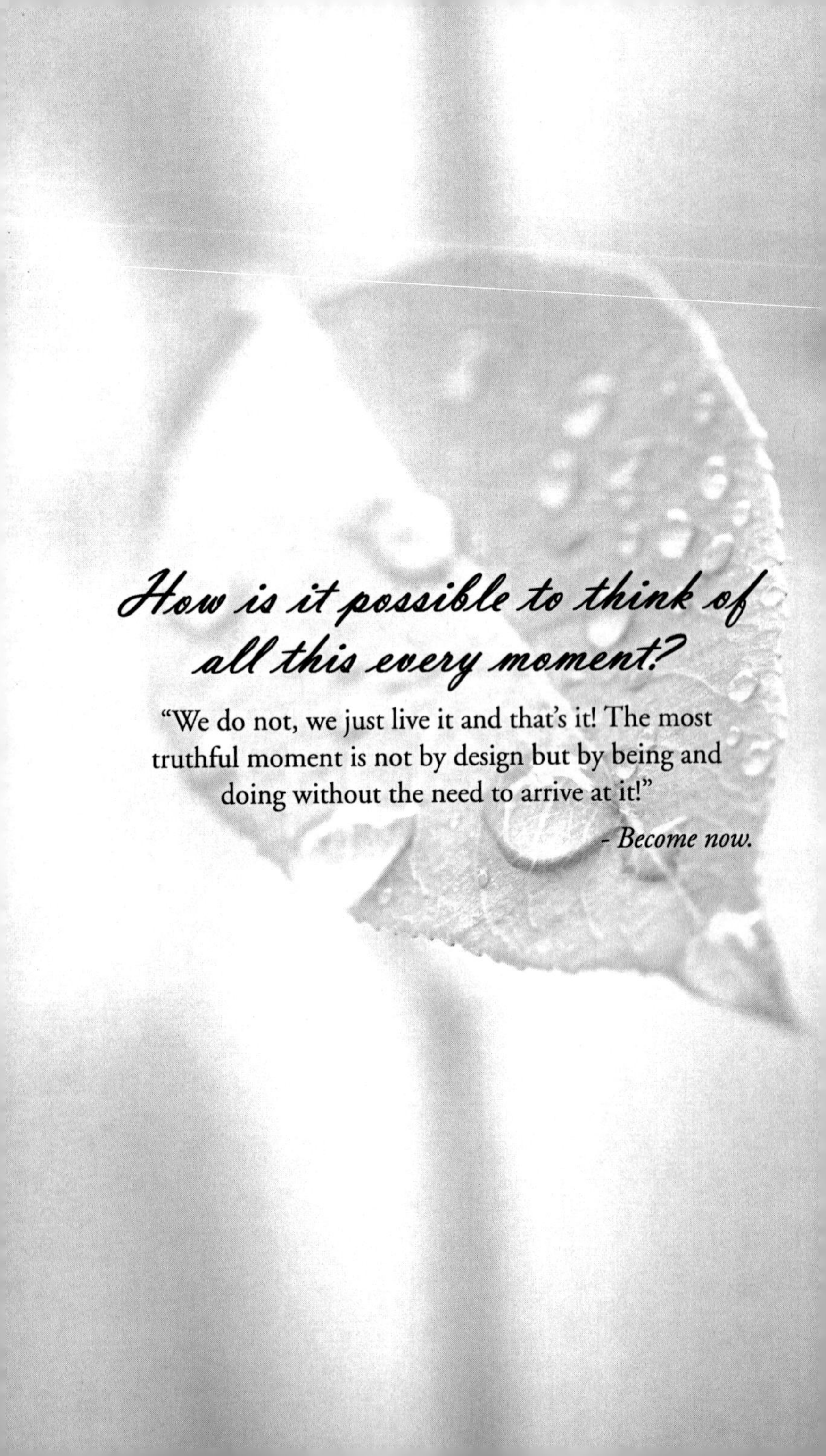

How is it possible to think of all this every moment?

"We do not, we just live it and that's it! The most truthful moment is not by design but by being and doing without the need to arrive at it!"

- Become now.

So, how does it help?

"A 'meaning-less' moment is the one fullest of life!"

- Because you're 'being here' without carrying the burden of the past or future reasoning.

I am so restless that I am never in the moment. So what?

"Good for you as long as you are having 'restless fun' in the journey towards the destination. Remember the stillness in the flow.

If I do not live in my moment, I might be craving for it, and yet carving out someone else's reality!"

- Else, we will be chasing happiness all our life.

How can we keep our dreams alive?

"All of us are magical musicians. All we need to do is, listen to the dream tunes within by silencing the noise of the reality master!"

- If we constantly feed the voices of reality, they will surely deflect us.

But what if we've tasted failure?

"We use the words 'what if it doesnt' so very often by standing outside the space of possibilities!"

- Let the past failures not kill the child within.

What about the 'ifs and buts?'

"Between all the 'ifs *and* buts' lie your *dreams*! Though I make an effort to bridge the gap, they together dilute my meaning. On my own however, I am abundant!"

- 'And'

- The 'ifs and buts' are cousins of the doubtful me. They stop us from taking that leap of faith.

Challenge — Possibility, lucky you! You have solutions to all the problems.

Possibility — Challenge, lucky you! You bring in a lot of questions. Without you I do not exist.

Result Master — I embrace the energy of your togetherness.

What do we mean by looking beyond?

"You can never look beyond; you need to be there.
Something truly new happens not by moving away from the old, but by foreseeing a shift from the new itself!"

- Step into the future, feel it and be afar it. Else, you'll color it with the present.

What drives a meaningful change?

"When we meet and embrace our reflection, it's time to look out for a new mirror!"

- When we are happy with what we've become, there is a drive to create new opportunities.

What does it take to root out the weeds?

"We need to stop somewhere; to start elsewhere!"

- Root out the old constraining belief patterns.

Your empty reflective space...
gift it!

PAINT YOUR CANVAS!

And what's the biggest hurdle?

"Everyone is busy with their 'battle for joy!'"

- Running after frivolous pleasures.

So, what do you suggest?

"Let it be as it was meant to be until…

…and

you will see the turnaround magic unfold!"

- Everything takes its own time to blossom…

So, what will help us keep going?

"Every moment is eternal if we believe that the magic is on!"

- It's one long lasting fun run, if we believe that life will pleasantly surprise us with wonderful gifts.

What does it take to plunge and forge ahead?

"It's only when we take that exploring plunge that the universe creates a new space to accommodate it. This ongoing urge is '*living*!'"

- The 'urge' to explore always meets with 'friendly opportunities' waiting to hug!

All said and done, isn't it important to be realistic?

"It is the energy of the flow that nourishes the game play between the conscious and the subconscious mind. Here is where the two shake hands. The true beauty manifests when the game play between the two begins!"

- The seamless bonding of intuition and logic creates a marvelous life dance.

I don't think all of us can achieve it. Can we?

"When you bump into the 'I deserve' paradigm in life, it offers new possibilities. You communicate to the universe that you are ready to receive and the magic unfolds.

This is not an overnight journey though. Few of us meet with it and few just don't!"

- What you feel you deserve, is what you'll seek.

But aren't you too a perception and not the absolute truth?

"You invited me and hence you know it better. All that you sense and acknowledge is 'your truth!'

Remember—what you allow your 'nature' to choose effortlessly is what you give and receive in abundance immensely!"

- Be yourself, feel lighter and fly high.

It was evening time and my inner master once again suggested that we step out for a breath of fresh air. As we stepped out, he looked into my eyes and said, "I would like to take you to the place where I reside."

We drove down to a place away from the hustle and bustle of the city. Along the way, the conversation that had gone by was ringing in my mind. After a drive of over an hour, we reached the place.

It was one of the most beautiful places I had visited recently. With lush green trees and open skies, nature had endowed its gift to the fullest. As we got off the car, we walked to a nearby cliff and after having covered a distance, within minutes I was standing on a beach just behind it. I could only hear the sound of the mighty sea waves and feel the vastness around. He then said, "I have brought you here to show your future."

I stood there silently staring at the horizon. It was a unique experience of being at peace with self. I then closed my eyes, took a deep breath and shouted with all the energy in my voice, "I am the stars, I am the awareness, I am joy, I am pain, I am magical, I am free and I am all of this '*now*!'"

And I do not recall the echo!

In that moment, I had hugged my inner master and the universal energy. I was serenely breathing in the present!

I had woken up feeling a new sense of liveliness I had derived from the same sea I had been staring at—the sea of life!

I realized that it happened because I had not only invited the newer me into my life, but was willing to let go of the older me.

As I lay on my bed, I saw a letter addressed to me that said, "See you the next time you need me. I will knock on the door once again when you call me with the same warmth. You have done it once and I trust you will keep these exchanges on!

Now, I am off to work on my next assignment. You set the stage and I will be around!"

29 December, 11:30 PM.

I had written this and saw the pen lying uncapped on the corner table. I was in two minds — should I cap it or should I not.

If I don't, the ink will dry up and if I do, then...

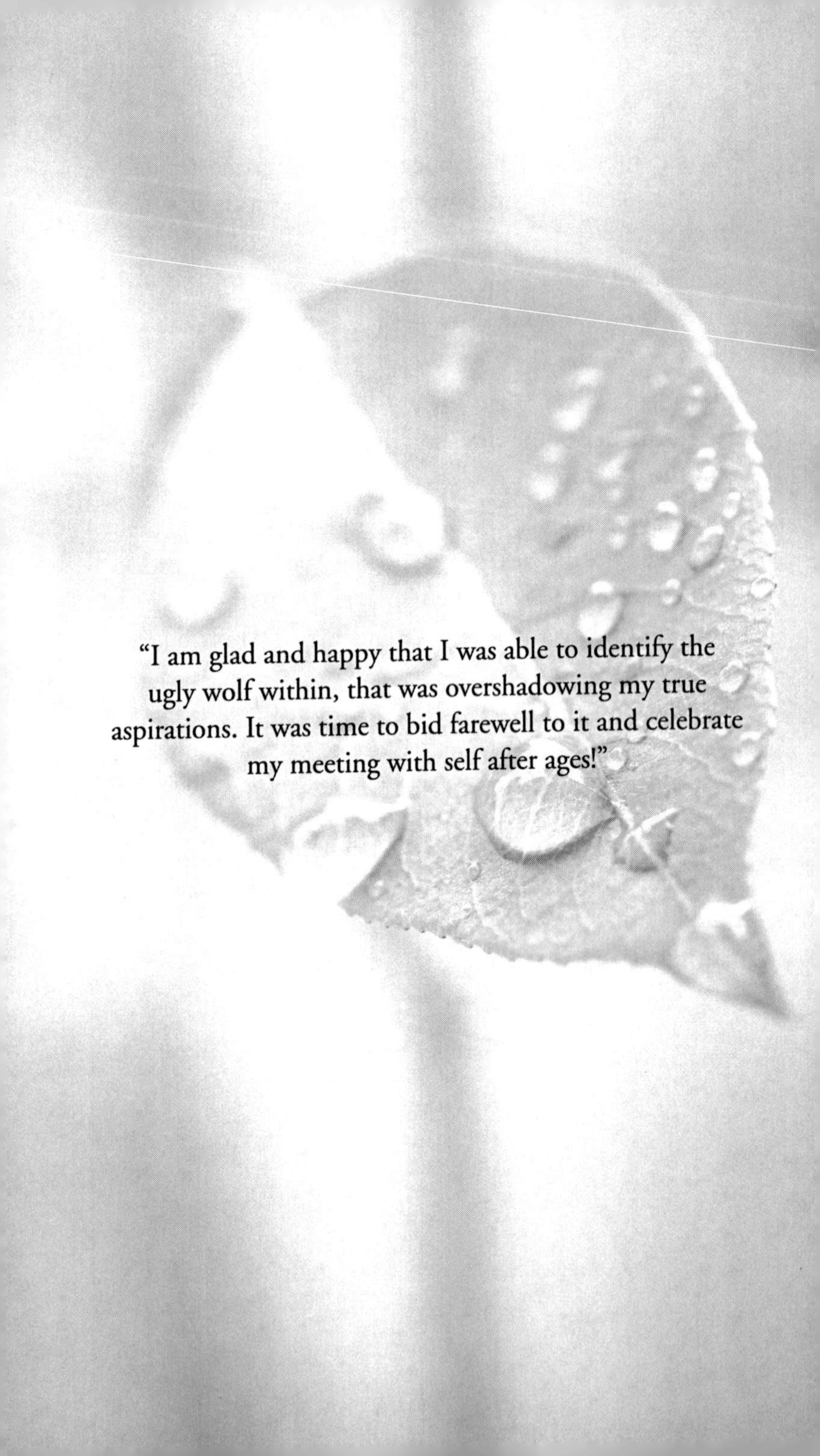

"I am glad and happy that I was able to identify the ugly wolf within, that was overshadowing my true aspirations. It was time to bid farewell to it and celebrate my meeting with self after ages!"

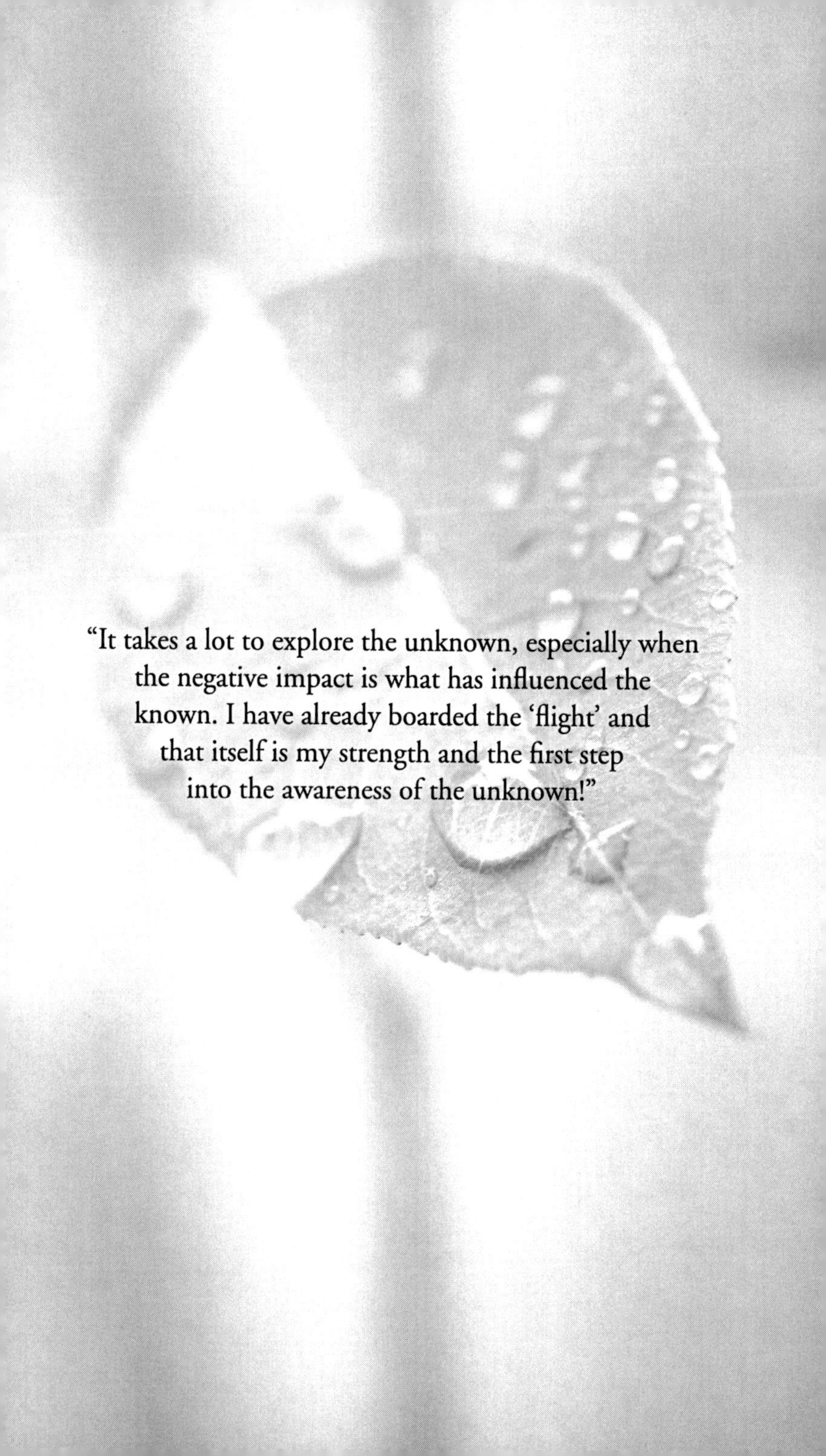

"It takes a lot to explore the unknown, especially when the negative impact is what has influenced the known. I have already boarded the 'flight' and that itself is my strength and the first step into the awareness of the unknown!"

"Going ahead, I have to *reflect, reflect* and *reflect* and not allow the reasoning and logic to come in the way. These two would appear as friends; however, they are the ones who will pamper the reality master and pull me back into the known comfortable space. They are often the most liked because they have solutions to their problems. However, presently, I do not need solutions but many questions in the visualization space!"

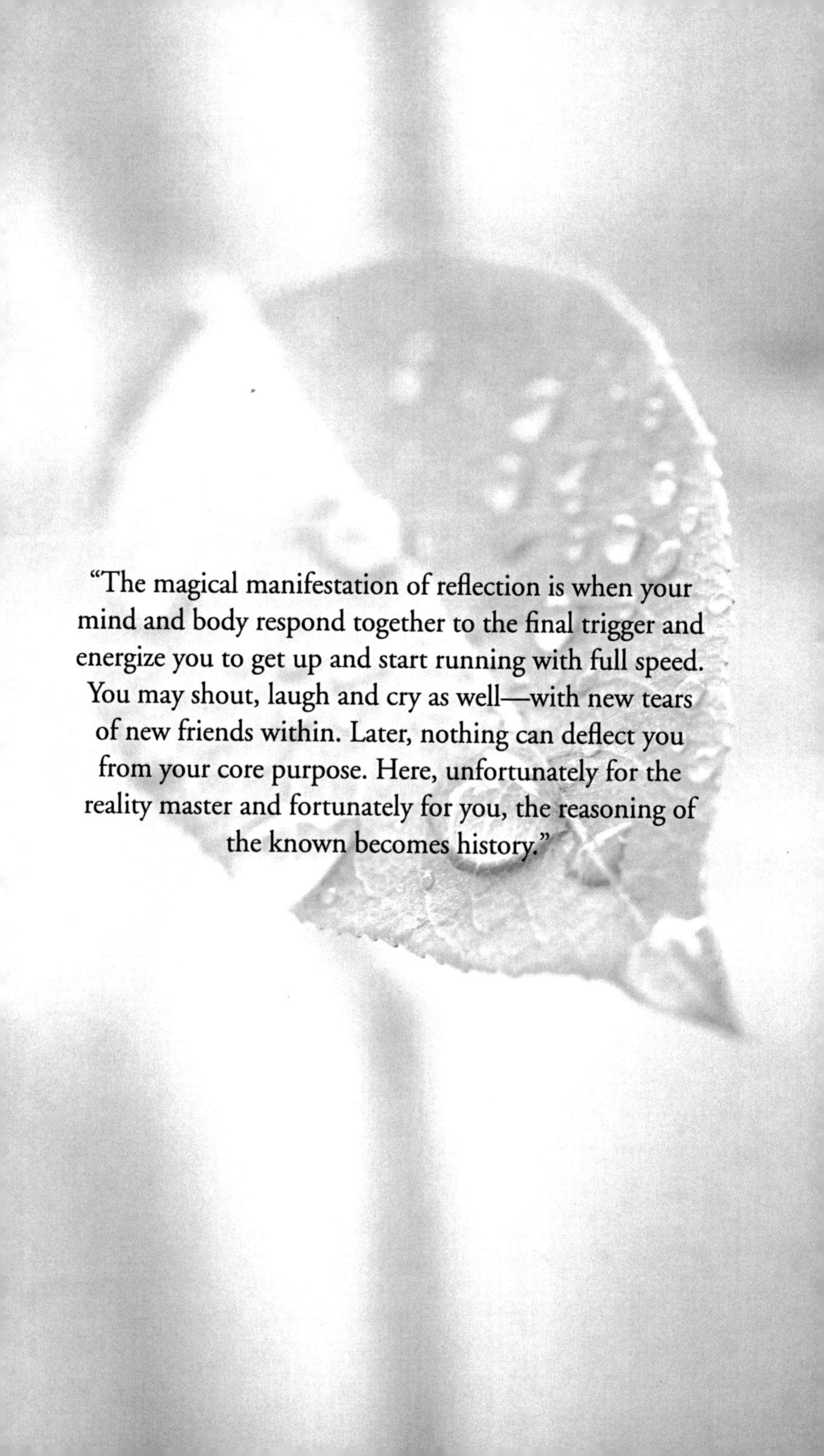

"The magical manifestation of reflection is when your mind and body respond together to the final trigger and energize you to get up and start running with full speed. You may shout, laugh and cry as well—with new tears of new friends within. Later, nothing can deflect you from your core purpose. Here, unfortunately for the reality master and fortunately for you, the reasoning of the known becomes history."

"Life is … Love is … the child within … *hug it!*"

“And the child in me said, ‘Just play the game!’”

"We bump into the different tunes of life, only when we are ready to go there and dance!"

"This conversation helped me meet a new friend—the 'liberated me'—the energy beyond the 'still noise' and the 'dynamic silence.' I could feel it like the cool breeze stepping in through the open windows of my house of self. The control of the breeze might not totally be in my hand; however, to keep the windows open or shut is surely my *choice*!"

"Dance to the tunes of the music called *life*!"

"Dance passionately and enjoy the tunes of your music!"

"Surprise yourself with new genres of the life dance!"

"Dance through the darkness to the light of dawn!"

"And here we are, back to where we started. Begin afresh with nothing … that's *life*!"

"Empty it!"

"A major thought breakthrough is just around the corner … *soar high*!"

"It needs to flash so fiercely in the mind's eye that you *act* on it with faith and commitment. And that is it!"

"Fill it!"

"Wishing you a 'wish-full' flight, I look forward to hearing about it once you land in your new space of *choice*!"

Thank you,
Life!